ROBINSON CRUSOE

Have you ever been alone for a long time? Could you live alone on an island for many years? Could you build yourself a house, learn to grow corn and make bread, learn to make your own clothes from animal skins?

Robinson Crusoe is bored with his quiet life at home in England. He decides to be a sailor, and to travel the seas of the world. He has many exciting adventures, and in 1659 he is in a ship sailing from Brazil to Africa. One day there is a terrible storm. The ship begins to break up, and soon Crusoe and his friends are fighting for their lives in an angry sea. All his friends die, but Crusoe lives and reaches land. He finds himself in a strange, wild country – alive, but alone on a small island, with no food, no boat, no way of escape.

He will be there for the next twenty-seven years . . .

OXFORD BOOKWORMS LIBRARY

Classics

Robinson Crusoe

Stage 2 (700 headwords)

Series Editor: Jennifer Bassett
Founder Editor: Tricia Hedge
Activities Editors: Jennifer Bassett and Alison Baxter

DANIEL DEFOE

The Life and
Strange Surprising Adventures of
Robinson Crusoe

Retold by
Diane Mowat

Illustrated by
Anthony Williams

OXFORD UNIVERSITY PRESS

OXFORD
UNIVERSITY PRESS

Great Clarendon Street, Oxford OX2 6DP

Oxford University Press is a department of the University of Oxford.
It furthers the University's objective of excellence in research, scholarship,
and education by publishing worldwide in

Oxford New York

Auckland Cape Town Dar es Salaam Hong Kong Karachi
Kuala Lumpur Madrid Melbourne Mexico City Nairobi
New Delhi Shanghai Taipei Toronto

With offices in

Argentina Austria Brazil Chile Czech Republic France Greece
Guatemala Hungary Italy Japan Poland Portugal Singapore
South Korea Switzerland Thailand Turkey Ukraine Vietnam

OXFORD and OXFORD ENGLISH are registered trade marks of
Oxford University Press in the UK and in certain other countries

ISBN 978 0 19 479070 3

A complete recording of this Bookworms edition of
Robinson Crusoe is available.

Printed in China

Maps by: Anthony Williams

Word count (main text): 6,830 words

For more information on the Oxford Bookworms Library,
visit www.oup.com/elt/gradedreaders

The manufacturer's authorised representative in the EU for product safety is
Oxford University Press España S.A. of el Parque Empresarial San Fernando de Henares,
Avenida de Castilla, 2 - 28830 Madrid (www.oup.es/en)

CONTENTS

1
My first sea journey

Before I begin my story, I would like to tell you a little about myself.

I was born in the year 1632, in the city of York in the north of England. My father was German, but he came to live and work in England. Soon after that, he married my mother, who was English. Her family name was Robinson, so, when I was born, they called me Robinson, after her.

My father did well in his business and I went to a good school. He wanted me to get a good job and live a quiet, comfortable life. But I didn't want that. I wanted adventure and an exciting life.

I wanted adventure and an exciting life.

1

'I want to be a sailor and go to sea,' I told my mother and father. They were very unhappy about this.

'Please don't go,' my father said. 'You won't be happy, you know. Sailors have a difficult and dangerous life.' And because I loved him, and he was unhappy, I tried to forget about the sea.

But I couldn't forget, and about a year later, I saw a friend in town. His father had a ship, and my friend said to me, 'We're sailing to London tomorrow. Why don't you come with us?'

And so, on September 1st, 1651, I went to Hull, and the next day we sailed for London.

But, a few days later, there was a strong wind. The sea was rough and dangerous, and the ship went up and down, up and down. I was very ill, and very afraid.

The sea was rough and dangerous.

'Oh, I don't want to die!' I cried. 'I want to live! If I live, I'll go home and never go to sea again!'

The next day the wind dropped, and the sea was quiet and beautiful again.

'Well, Bob,' my friend laughed. 'How do you feel now? The wind wasn't too bad.'

'What!' I cried. 'It was a terrible storm.'

'Oh, that wasn't a storm,' my friend answered. 'Just a little wind. Forget it. Come and have a drink.'

After a few drinks with my friend, I felt better. I forgot about the danger and decided not to go home. I didn't want my friends and family to laugh at me!

I stayed in London for some time, but I still wanted to go to sea. So, when the captain of a ship asked me to go with him to Guinea in Africa, I agreed. And so I went to sea for the second time.

It was a good ship and everything went well at first, but I was very ill again. Then, when we were near the Canary Islands, a Turkish pirate ship came after us. They were famous thieves of the sea at that time. There was a long, hard fight, but when it finished, we and the ship were prisoners.

The Turkish captain and his men took us to Sallee in Morocco. They wanted to sell us as slaves in the markets there. But in the end the Turkish captain decided to keep me for himself, and took me home with him. This was a sudden and terrible change in my life. I was now a slave and this Turkish captain was my master.

2
Down the coast of Africa

For two long years I lived the life of a slave. I worked in the house and the garden, and every day I planned to escape, but it was never possible. I thought about it day and night. My master liked to go fishing in a little boat, and he always took me with him. A man called Moely, and a young boy also went with us.

One day my master said to us, 'Some of my friends want to go fishing tomorrow. Get the boat ready.'

So we put a lot of food and drink on the boat, and the next morning, we waited for my master and his friends. But when my master arrived, he was alone.

'My friends don't want to go fishing today,' he said to me. 'But you go with Moely and the boy, and catch some fish for our supper tonight.'

'Yes, master,' I answered quietly, but inside I was excited. 'Perhaps now I can escape,' I said to myself.

My master went back to his friends and we took the boat out to sea. For a time we fished quietly, and then I moved carefully behind Moely and knocked him into the water. 'Swim!' I cried. 'Swim to the shore!'

My master liked to shoot seabirds and so there were guns on the boat. Quickly, I took one of these guns. Moely was swimming after the boat and I shouted to him:

'Go back to the shore! You can swim there – it's not too far. I won't hurt you, but if you come near the boat, I'll shoot you through the head!' So Moely turned, and swam back to the shore as quickly as he could.

'Swim back to the shore!' I shouted.

Then I said to the boy, 'Xury, if you help me, I'll be a good friend to you. If you don't help me, I'll push you into the sea too.'

But Xury was happy to help me. 'I'll go all over the world with you,' he cried.

I wanted to sail to the Canary Islands, but I was afraid to go too far from the shore. It was only a small boat. And so we sailed on south for some days. We had very little water, and it was dangerous country here, with many wild animals. We were afraid, but we often had to go on shore to get more water. Once I used a gun to shoot a wild animal. I don't know what animal it was, but it made a good meal.

For about ten or twelve days we sailed on south, down the coast of Africa. Then one day we saw some people on the shore – strange, wild people, who did not look friendly. By now we had very little food, and we really needed help. We were afraid, but we had to go on shore.

At first, they were afraid of us, too. Perhaps white people never visited this coast. We did not speak their language, of course, so we used our hands and faces to show that we were hungry. They came with food for us, but then they moved away quickly. We carried the food to our boat, and they watched us. I tried to thank them, but I had nothing to give them.

Just then two big wild cats came down to the shore

They gave us food and water.

from the mountains. I think they were leopards. The people were afraid of these wild cats, and the women cried out. Quickly, I took a gun, and shot one of the animals. The second wild cat ran back up into the mountains.

Guns were new to these African people, and they were afraid of the loud noise and the smoke. But they were happy about the dead wild cat. I gave them the meat of the dead animal, and they gave us more food and water.

We now had a lot of food and water, and we sailed on. Eleven days later we came near the Cape Verde Islands. We could see them, but we couldn't get near because there was no wind. We waited.

Suddenly Xury called to me, 'Look, a ship!'

He was right! We called and shouted and sailed our little boat as fast as we could. But the ship did not see us.

8

Then I remembered the guns which made a lot of smoke.

Then I remembered the guns which made a lot of smoke. A few minutes later the ship saw us and turned.

When we were on the ship, the Portuguese captain listened to my story. He was going to Brazil and agreed to help me, but he wanted nothing for his help. 'No,' he said, when I tried to pay him. 'Perhaps, one day, someone will help *me* when I need it.'

But he gave me money for my boat, and for Xury, too. At first, I did not want to sell Xury as a slave, after all our dangerous adventures together. But Xury was happy to go to the captain, and the captain was a good man. 'In ten years' time,' he said, 'Xury can go free.'

When we arrived in Brazil three weeks later, I said goodbye to the captain and Xury, left the ship, and went to begin a new life.

3
The storm and the shipwreck

I stayed in Brazil and worked hard for some years. By then I was rich . . . but also bored. One day some friends came to me and said, 'We're going to Africa to do business. Why don't you come with us? We'll all be rich after this journey!'

How stupid I was! I had an easy, comfortable life in Brazil, but, of course, I agreed. And so, in 1659, I went to sea again.

At first, all went well, but then there was a terrible storm. For twelve days the wind and the rain didn't stop. We lost three men in the sea, and soon the ship had holes in its sides. 'We're all going to die this time,' I said to myself. Then one morning one of the sailors saw land, but the next minute our ship hit some sand just under the sea. The ship could not move and we were really in danger now. The sea was trying to break the ship into pieces, and we had very little time. Quickly, we put a boat into the sea and got off the ship. But the sea was

One of the sailors saw land.

very rough and our little boat could not live for long in that wild water.

Half an hour later the angry sea turned our boat over and we were all in the water. I looked round for my friends, but I could see nobody. I was alone.

I fell on the wet sand.

That day I was lucky, and the sea carried me to the shore. I could not see the land, only mountains of water all around me. Then, suddenly, I felt the ground under my feet. Another mountain of water came, pushed me up the beach, and I fell on the wet sand.

At first I was very thankful to be alive. Slowly, I got to my feet and went higher up the shore. From there, I looked out to sea. I could see our ship, but it was wrecked and there was nobody near it. There was nobody in the water. All my friends were dead. I was alive, but in a strange wild country, with no food, no water, and no gun.

It was dark now and I was tired. I was afraid to sleep on the shore. Perhaps there were wild animals there. So I went up into a tree and I stayed there all night.

4
A new life on an island

When day came, the sea was quiet again. I looked for our ship and, to my surprise, it was still there and still in one piece. 'I think I can swim to it,' I said to myself. So I walked down to the sea and before long, I was at the ship and was swimming round it. But how could I get on to it? In the end, I got in through a hole in the side, but it wasn't easy.

There was a lot of water in the ship, but the sand under the sea was still holding the ship in one place. The back of the ship was high out of the water, and I was very thankful for this because all the ship's food was there. I was very hungry so I began to eat something at once.

Then I decided to take some of it back to the shore with me. But how could I get it there?

I looked around the ship, and after a few minutes, I found some long pieces of wood. I tied them together with rope. Then I got the things that I wanted

I tied the pieces of wood together with rope.

I took many tools.

from the ship. There was a big box of food – rice, and salted meat, and hard ship's bread. I also took many strong knives and other tools, the ship's sails and ropes, paper, pens, books, and seven guns. Now I needed a little sail from the ship, and then I was ready. Slowly and carefully, I went back to the shore. It was difficult to stop my things from falling into the sea, but in the end I got everything on to the shore.

Now I needed somewhere to keep my things.

There were some hills around me, so I decided to build myself a little house on one of them. I walked to the top of the highest hill and looked down. I was very unhappy, because I saw then that I was on an island. There were two smaller islands a few miles away, and after that, only the sea. Just the sea, for mile after mile after mile.

After a time, I found a little cave in the side of a hill. In front of it, there was a good place to make a home. So, I used the ship's sails, rope, and pieces of wood, and after a lot of hard work I had a very fine tent. The cave at the back of my tent was a good place to keep my food, and so I called it my 'kitchen'. That night, I went to sleep in my new home.

The next day I thought about the possible dangers on the island. Were there wild animals, and perhaps wild people too, on my island? I didn't know, but I was very afraid. So I decided to build a very strong fence. I cut down young trees and put them in the ground, in a half-circle around the front of my tent. I used many of the ship's ropes too, and in the end my fence was as strong as a stone wall. Nobody could get over it, through it, or round it.

Making tents and building fences is hard work. I needed many tools to help me. So I decided to go back to the ship again, and get some more things.

I went back twelve times, but soon after my twelfth

The fence round my tent was as strong as a stone wall.

visit there was another terrible storm. The next morning, when I looked out to sea, there was no ship.

When I saw that, I was very unhappy. 'Why am I alive, and why are all my friends dead?' I asked myself. 'What will happen to me now, alone on this island without friends? How can I ever escape from it?'

Then I told myself that I was lucky – lucky to be alive, lucky to have food and tools, lucky to be young and strong. But I knew that my island was somewhere off the coast of South America. Ships did not often come down this coast, and I said to myself, 'I'm going to be on this island for a long time.' So, on a long piece of wood, I cut these words:

I CAME HERE ON 30TH SEPTEMBER 1659

After that, I decided to make a cut for each day.

5
Learning to live alone

I still needed a lot of things. 'Well,' I said, 'I'm going to have to make them.' So, every day, I worked.

First of all, I wanted to make my cave bigger. I carried out stone from the cave, and after many days' hard work I had a large cave in the side of the hill. Then I needed a table and a chair, and that was my next job. I had to work on them for a long time. I also wanted to make places to put all my food, and all my tools and guns. But every time I wanted a piece of wood, I had to cut down a tree. It was long, slow, difficult work, and during the next months I learnt to be very clever with my tools. There was no hurry. I had all the time in the world.

I also went out every day, and I always had my gun with me. Sometimes I killed a wild animal, and then I had meat to eat.

But when it got dark, I had to go to bed because I had no light. I couldn't read or write because I couldn't see. For a long time, I didn't know what to do. But in the end, I learnt how to use the fat of dead animals to make a light.

The weather on my island was usually very hot, and there were often storms and heavy rain. The next June, it rained all the time, and I couldn't go out very often. I was also ill for some weeks, but slowly, I got better. When I was stronger, I began to go out again. The first time I killed a wild animal, and the second time I caught a big turtle.

I caught a big turtle.

17

I was on the island for ten months before I visited other parts of it. During those months I worked hard on my cave and my house and my fence. Now I was ready to find out more about the rest of the island.

First, I walked along the side of a little river. There, I found open ground without trees. Later, I came to more trees with many different fruits. I decided to take a lot of the fruit, and to put it to dry in the sun for a time. Then I could keep it for many months.

That night I went to sleep in a tree for the second time, and the next day I went on with my journey. Soon I came to an opening in the hills. In front of me, everything was green, and there were flowers everywhere. There were also a lot of different birds and animals. I saw that my house was on the worst side of the island. But I didn't want to move from there. It was my home now. I stayed away for three days, and then I came home. But I often went back to the other, greener side of the island.

And so my life went on. Every month I learnt to do or to make something new. But I had troubles and accidents too. Once there was a terrible storm with very heavy rain. The roof of my cave fell in, and nearly killed me! I had to build it up again with many pieces of wood.

I had a lot of food now. I cooked it over a fire or dried it in the sun. So I always had meat during the rainy months when I could not go out with a gun. I learnt to make pots to keep my food in. But I wanted very much to make a harder, stronger pot – a pot that would not break in a fire. I tried many times, but I could not do it. Then one day I was lucky. I made some new pots and put them in a very hot fire. They changed colour, but did

My first pot

not break. I left them there for many hours, and when they were cold again, I found that they were hard and strong. That night I was very happy. I had hot water for the first time on the island.

By then, I also had my own bread. That was luck, too. One day I found a little bag. We used it on the ship, to

My first cornfield

keep the chickens' food in. There was still some of the food in the bag, and I dropped some of it onto the ground. A month later I saw something bright green there, and after six months I had a very small field of corn. I was very excited. Perhaps now I could make my own bread!

It was easy to say, but not so easy to do. It is a lot of work to

19

make bread from corn. Many people eat bread, but how many people can take corn from a field and make bread out of it without help? I had to learn and to make many new things, and it was a year before I cooked and ate my first bread.

During all this time I never stopped thinking about escape. When I travelled across to the other side of the island, I could see the other islands, and I said to myself, 'Perhaps I can get there with a boat. Perhaps I can get back to England one day.'

So I decided to make myself a boat. I cut down a big tree, and then began to make a long hole in it. It was hard work, but about six months later, I had a very fine canoe.

Next, I had to get it down to the sea. How stupid I was! Why didn't I think before I began work? Of course, the canoe was too heavy. I couldn't move it! I pulled and pushed and tried everything, but it didn't move. I was very unhappy for a long time after that.

That happened in my fourth year on the island. In my sixth year I did make myself a smaller canoe, but I did not try to escape in it. The boat was too small for a long journey, and I did not want to die at sea. The island was my home now, not my prison, and I was just happy to be alive. A year or two later, I made myself a second canoe on the other side of the island. I also built myself a second house there, and so I had two homes.

Of course, the canoe was too heavy. I couldn't move it!

My life was still busy from morning to night. There were always things to do or to make. I learnt to make new clothes for myself from the skins of dead animals. They looked very strange, it is true, but they kept me dry in the rain.

I kept food and tools at both my houses, and also wild goats. There were many goats on the island, and I made fields with high fences to keep them in. They learnt to take food from me, and soon I had goat's milk to drink every day. I also worked hard in my cornfields. And so many years went by.

Soon I had goat's milk to drink.

6
A *footprint*

Then, one year, something strange and terrible happened. I often walked along the shore, and one day I saw something in the sand. I went over to look at it more carefully, and stopped in sudden surprise.

It was a footprint – the footprint of a man!

Who could this be? Afraid, I looked around me. I listened. I waited. Nothing. I was more and more afraid. Perhaps this

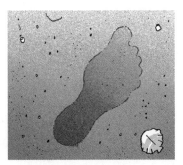

It was a footprint!

man was one of those wild people who killed and ate other men! I looked everywhere, but there was nobody, and no other footprint. I turned and hurried home. 'There's someone on my island,' I said to myself. 'Perhaps he knows about me . . . Perhaps he's watching me now from behind a tree . . . Perhaps he wants to kill me.'

That night I couldn't sleep. The next day I got all my guns ready and I put more wood and young trees around my house. Nobody could see me now. But, after fifteen years alone on the island, I was afraid, and I did not leave my cave for three days.

In the end, I had to go out to milk my goats. But for two years I was afraid. I stayed near my home and I never used my guns because I didn't want to make a noise. I could not forget the footprint, but I saw and heard nothing more, and slowly I began to feel happier.

One day, a year later, I was over on the west side of the island. From there I could see the other islands, and I could also see a boat, far out to sea. 'If you have a boat,' I thought, 'it's easy to sail across to this island. Perhaps that explains the footprint – it was a visitor from one of the other islands.'

I began to move more freely around the island again, and built myself a third house. It was a very secret place in a cave. 'No wild man will ever find that,' I said to myself.

Then one year something happened which I can never forget. I was again on the west side of the island and was walking along the shore. Suddenly, I saw something which made me feel ill. There were heads, arms, feet, and other pieces of men's bodies everywhere. For a minute, I couldn't think, and then I understood. Sometimes there were fights between the wild men on the other islands. Then they came here to my island with their prisoners, to kill them, cook them, and eat them. Slowly, I went home, but I was very angry. How could men do this?

For many months I watched carefully for the smoke

from fires, but I didn't see anything. Somehow the wild men came and went, and I never saw them. I was angry and afraid. I wanted to shoot them all, but there were many of them and only one of me. 'Perhaps I can shoot two or three,' I said to myself, 'but then they will kill and eat me.'

Then, one morning in my twenty-third year on the island, I was out in my fields and I saw the smoke from a fire. Quickly, I went up the hill to watch.

There were nine men around the fire, and they were cooking their terrible food. Then these wild men danced round the fire, singing and shouting. This went on for

The wild men danced round the fire, singing and shouting.

25

about two hours, and then they got into their boats and sailed away. I went down to the shore and saw the blood of the dead men on the sand. 'The next time they come, I'm going to kill them,' I said angrily.

7
Man Friday

For two years I never went anywhere without my gun. I felt lonely and afraid, and had many sleepless nights. One night there was a very bad storm, and I thought I heard the sound of guns out at sea. The next morning I looked out, and saw a ship. It was lying on its side not far from the shore. Quickly, I put my little boat in the water and sailed out to it.

There were two dead men on the ship, but no one alive. The bodies of the other sailors were lost in the sea. I took some clothes and tools, and also a box of Spanish gold and silver money. I was a rich man now, but what use was money to me? I could not buy anything with it.

What use was money to me?

26

I wanted people, a friend, somebody to talk to . . . somebody who could help me escape from my island. One morning I woke up and made a plan. 'I'll try to catch one of the prisoners of the wild men,' I said to myself. 'He'll be happy to be alive and perhaps he'll help me to escape.' I watched day and night, but for a year and a half there were no boats.

Then one day five boats came. There were about thirty men and they had two prisoners. They made their fire on the sand and danced round it. Then they killed one of the prisoners and began to cook their terrible meal. The second prisoner waited under the trees, with two men to watch him. Suddenly, the prisoner turned and ran. The two men ran after him, but the other wild men were busy round the fire and did not see what was happening.

The prisoner ran like a wild goat, and soon I saw that he was coming near the bottom of my hill. As fast as I could, I ran down the hill and jumped out of the trees between the prisoner and the two wild men. I hit the first man with the wooden end of my gun and he fell down, but I had to shoot the second man. The poor prisoner did not move. He was afraid of the noise of my gun.

I called to him and tried to show him that I was friendly. Slowly, he moved nearer to me, but just then the first wild man began to get up from the ground. Then the prisoner spoke and I understood that he wanted my sword. How happy I was to hear words again! I gave him my sword, and at once he cut off the head of his enemy.

Hurriedly, we hid the dead bodies under some leaves,

I gave him my sword.

and then left quickly. I took my prisoner to my secret cave on the other side of the island and gave him food and drink. After that, he went to sleep.

He was a fine young man, about twenty-five years old, tall and well-built, with a kind face and a nice smile. He had a brown skin, black hair, bright eyes and strong white teeth. I decided to give him the name of 'Man Friday', because I first saw him on a Friday.

When he woke up in the morning, he ran out to me. I was milking my goats in the field, and he got down on the ground and put his head near my foot. I understood that he was thanking me, and I tried to show him that I was his friend.

I began to teach him to speak English, and soon he could say his name, 'Master', and 'Yes' and 'No'. How good it was to hear a man's voice again!

Later that day we went back to my first house. We went carefully along the beach, but there were no boats and no wild men. Just blood and bones all over the sand. I felt

There were bones all over the sand.

ill, but Friday wanted to eat the pieces of men's bodies which were still on the ground. I showed him that this was terrible for me, and he understood.

When we got to my house, I gave Man Friday some trousers, and I made him a coat and a hat. He liked his new clothes very much. Then I made him a little tent to sleep in, but for a few weeks I always took my gun to bed with me. Perhaps Friday was still a wild man and would try to kill me in the night. At first, Friday was very afraid of my gun. Sometimes he talked to it, and asked it not to kill him.

Friday was a quick learner and his English got better day by day. He helped me with the goats and with the work in the cornfields, and soon we were good friends. I enjoyed teaching him and, most of all, having a friend to talk to. This was the happiest of all my years on the island.

Friday and I lived together happily for three years. I told him the story of my adventures and about life in England, and he told me about his country and his people. One day we were at the top of the highest hill on the island, and we were looking out to sea. It was a very clear day and we could see a long way. Suddenly, Friday began to jump up and down, very excited.

'What's the matter?' I said.

'Look, Master, look!' Friday cried. 'I can see my country. Look over there!'

I looked, and there to the north-west, between the sea and the sky, was a long thin piece of land. I learnt later that it was the island of Trinidad, and that my island was in the mouth of the River Orinoco on the north coast of South America.

I began to think again about escape. Perhaps Friday wanted to go home too. Perhaps together we could get to his country. But what then? Would Friday still be my friend, or would his people kill me and eat me?

I took Friday to the other side of the island and showed him my big canoe. It still lay under the trees. It was very old now, and there were holes in the wood.

'Could a boat like this sail to your country, Friday?' I asked him.

'Oh yes,' he answered. 'A boat like this can carry a lot of food and drink.'

'Then we'll make another canoe like it, and you can go home in it,' I said.

But Friday looked very unhappy. 'Why are you angry with me?' he asked. 'What have I done? Why do you want to send me home?'

'But I thought you wanted to go home,' I said.

'Yes. But you must come with me. Kill me if you want, but don't send me away from you!'

Then I saw that Friday was a true friend, and so I agreed to go with him. We began work on the canoe at once. Friday chose the tree himself – he understood wood better than I did – and we cut it down. We worked hard and in a month the boat was finished. Two weeks later it was in the sea, and we began to get ready for our long journey.

8
Escape from the island

I was now in my twenty-seventh year on the island, and I did not want to be there for another year. We worked hard to get the corn in, and to make a lot of bread. We had dried fruit and salted meat, and big pots to keep water in. One evening Friday went out to look for a turtle for meat and eggs. But in less than an hour he was back, and he looked very afraid.

'Master! Master!' he cried. 'There's a great ship near the island, and men are coming to the shore in a boat!'

'There's a great ship near the island!'

I jumped up and ran with him down to the shore. To my great surprise, I saw that it was an English ship! But why was it here? English ships never came this way. Perhaps they were pirates! 'Don't let them see you, Friday!' I called. 'We'll hide in the trees and watch.'

There were eleven men in the boat, but three of them were prisoners. Their arms were tied with rope, but their legs were free and they could walk. The other sailors pushed the three prisoners up the beach, laughing and shouting and hitting them. Then some of them sat down on the sand and began to drink. Others walked away to look at the island, and two men stayed to watch the boat. The three prisoners walked slowly along the beach and sat down under a tree, not far from us. They looked very unhappy.

Very quietly, I came up behind them through the trees, and called out to them in English.

'Don't be afraid,' I said. 'I'm an Englishman. Perhaps I can help you.'

The three men turned and looked at me. They did not answer at once; they were too surprised. Perhaps they thought I was a wild man myself, in my strange home-made clothes of animals' skins, and with my long hair and beard. Then the oldest man spoke.

'I am the captain of that ship,' he said, 'and these two men are my first and second officers. Last night there was

*Perhaps they thought I was a wild man myself,
with my long hair and beard.*

a mutiny, and the seamen took the ship from me. Now
they're going to leave the three of us here, to die on this
island.'

'Do these mutineers have guns?'

'Only two,' he answered, 'and they've left those on
the boat.'

'All right,' I said. 'We'll fight them, but if we get your
ship back for you, you must take me back to England.'

The captain agreed immediately and thanked me very
warmly for his help. Friday ran back to my house to get
all the guns, and the captain and I made a plan.

The first part was easy because the seamen were not ready for a fight. We shot the two men at the boat, and the captain shot another man. This man, Tom Smith, was the worst of them all and he began the mutiny on the ship. Then the captain talked to the other five men, and they agreed to help him. They did not really want to be mutineers, but they were afraid of Tom Smith.

'Now,' I said to the captain, 'we must get back your ship. How many men are on it?'

'Twenty-six,' the captain replied, 'and they will fight hard because they won't want to go home. It is death for all mutineers in England. But not all the men are bad. I'm sure that some of them will help me.'

Just then we saw another boat, which was coming from the ship to the shore. There were ten men in it, and they all had guns. We ran into the trees and waited.

It was a long hard fight, but by now it was dark and this helped us very much. We ran here and there in the trees, calling and shouting. The seamen could not see us and did not know how many men they were fighting. In the end the first officer shouted to them:

'Put down your guns and stop fighting! The captain has fifty island people to help him. We can kill you all!'

So the seamen stopped fighting and we took their guns. Three of the men agreed to come back to the captain, and we put the others in my cave. Friday and I

It was a long hard fight.

stayed to watch the prisoners, while the captain and his men went back to fight for the ship.

All night we listened to the sound of guns and shouting, but in the morning, when the sun came up, the captain was master of his ship again. I went down to the shore to meet him.

'My dear friend,' he cried. 'There's your ship! I'll take you to the ends of the world in it!'

I put my arms round him, and we laughed and cried together. How happy I was to leave the island!

'I'll take you to the ends of the world!' cried the captain.

My good friend Friday came with me, of course, but we left the mutineers on the island. We decided not to kill them; they could begin a new life on the island. I showed them my three houses, my cornfields and my goats, and all my tools. Their life would be easy because of all my hard work for so many years.

And so, on the nineteenth of December 1686 – after twenty-seven years, two months and nineteen days – I said goodbye to my island and sailed home to England.

9
Home in England

When I came back to England, I felt like a stranger in the country. Many things were different, and not many people remembered me. I went home to York, but my father and mother were dead, and also my two brothers. I did find the two sons of one of my brothers. They were happy to learn that I was alive, and I was pleased to find some family.

After some months I decided to go down to Lisbon in Portugal. I had friends there who could help me to sell my land in Brazil, and I needed the money. Friday came with me. He was always a good and true friend to me.

In Lisbon I found the Portuguese captain, who took me in his ship to Brazil, all those years ago. It was good to see him again, and he helped me with my business.

Soon I was ready to go home again – by land. No more adventures and dangers by sea for me!

It was a long, hard journey. We had to cross the mountains between Spain and France in winter, and the snow was deep. Poor Friday was very afraid of the snow. In his country it was always hot, and he did not like cold weather.

Poor Friday was very afraid of the snow.

Back in England I found a house and began to live a quiet life. My two nephews came to live with me. The younger one wanted to be a sailor, and so I found him a place on a ship. After a while I married, and had three children, two sons and a daughter. Then my wife died, and my nephew, who was now the captain of a ship, came home to see me. He knew that I did not really like a quiet life.

'I have a fine ship, uncle,' he said. 'I'm going out to the East Indies – India, Malaya, the Philippines . . . Why don't you come with me?'

'I have a fine ship, uncle,' my nephew said.

And so, in 1694, I went to sea again, and had many more adventures. Perhaps one day I'll write another book about them.

GLOSSARY

captain   the most important person on a ship

coast   land which is near the sea

dry   the opposite of 'wet'

great   very big

master   the man who you work for and who is more important than you

mutineer   somebody who takes part in a mutiny

mutiny   when sailors fight and take the ship from the captain and officers

nephew   the son of your brother or sister

officer   an important person on a ship who works with the captain

pirate   someone who sails on the sea and steals from other ships

roof   the top of a building, over your head

shipwreck   an accident when a ship breaks up in a storm or on the rocks

shore   the ground where the land and sea meet

slave   a person who belongs to a master and who is given no money for his work

uncle   your mother's or your father's brother

wreck   to break something completely

Robinson Crusoe

ACTIVITIES

ACTIVITIES

Before Reading

1 **Read the story introduction on the first page, and the back cover. What do you know now about this story? Tick one box for each sentence.**

	YES	NO
1 Robinson Crusoe has a boring life.	☐	☐
2 He is in a ship sailing from South America when there is a terrible storm.	☐	☐
3 All his friends die in the shipwreck.	☐	☐
4 When he arrives on the island, he meets some other people.	☐	☐
5 One day he finds a footprint in the sand.	☐	☐
6 He leaves the island after fifteen years.	☐	☐

2 **What is going to happen in this story? Can you guess? Tick one box for each sentence.**

	YES	NO
1 Crusoe learns to grow corn and make bread.	☐	☐
2 He builds himself a boat and sails away.	☐	☐
3 He is often very hungry on the island.	☐	☐
4 The man who left the footprint is an enemy.	☐	☐
5 The footprint was made by someone who was also shipwrecked on the island.	☐	☐
6 Finding the footprint changes Crusoe's life.	☐	☐

44

ACTIVITIES
_____

While Reading

Read Chapters 1 to 3. Choose the best question-word for these questions, and then answer them. Use the map on page 4 to help you.

What / *Where*

1 ... happened to Crusoe when he sailed to London?
2 ... did he go when he left London?
3 ... was the ship when the pirate ship came after it?
4 ... did the Turkish pirate captain take Crusoe?
5 ... was the sudden and terrible change in Crusoe's life?
6 ... did Crusoe and Xury go when they escaped?
7 ... did the African people give Crusoe and Xury?
8 ... was the Portuguese captain going?
9 ... did Crusoe's friends want to go to get rich?
10 ... happened to the ship in the storm?
11 ... did the sea carry Crusoe?
12 ... did Crusoe sleep that first night?

Before you read Chapter 4 (*A new life on an island*), can you guess what Crusoe finds on the island?

1 A box of gold	4 Food and water
2 An empty old house	5 Pirates
3 Wild animals	6 A cave

Read Chapters 4 and 5. How did Crusoe live on the island? Make sentences from this table.

	fire a tent clothes the sun lights a canoe wood fields corn	to make a table. from a big tree. to make bread. to make strong pots. from animals' skins. to dry fruit and meat. from the ship's sails. to keep wild goats in. to build fences. from animals' fat.
He made He used		

Before you read Chapter 6 (*A footprint*), can you guess the answers to these questions?

1 Where does Crusoe find the footprint?
   a) in a field   b) on the shore   c) outside his house
2 Who made the footprint?
   a) a pirate   b) a wild man   c) a shipwrecked sailor

Read Chapters 6 and 7. Are these sentences true (T) or false (F)? Rewrite the false ones with the correct information.

1 Crusoe was very afraid of the wild men at first.
2 The wild men came to the island to kill and eat turtles.
3 Crusoe helped Man Friday to escape from the wild men.

4 Friday made Crusoe some clothes and a tent.

5 Friday wanted to go home to Trinidad alone.

6 Crusoe and Friday made a new canoe for their escape.

Before you read Chapter 8, can you guess how Crusoe and Friday escape from the island? Choose one of these ideas.

1 They sail to Trinidad in the canoe.

2 They sail back to England in an English ship.

3 They fight some pirates and take their ship.

Read Chapters 8 and 9, and then put these sentences in the right order.

1 The captain told Crusoe that the mutineers planned to leave him and his officers on the island to die.

2 Back in England, Crusoe got married and had a family.

3 Crusoe was very surprised when an English ship arrived.

4 Because of this, the captain was very happy to take Crusoe and Friday home.

5 So Crusoe sailed with him, and had more adventures.

6 Eleven men from the ship came to the shore in a boat, but the captain and his two officers were prisoners.

7 But later, his nephew planned to sail to the East Indies.

8 So Crusoe and Friday helped the captain to fight the mutineers and get back his ship.

After Reading

1 **Use the words below to complete this page from Robinson Crusoe's diary. (Use each word once.)**

catch, fat, fences, fishing, gun, happy, holes, home, raining, salted, shoot, skins, stronger, tree, wood

5TH AUGUST 1669:   At last it has stopped _____! This morning I cut down a _____ because I need more _____. The goats have broken two _____ already, so I must make them _____. Later, I went out _____ in my canoe, but I didn't _____ anything. For dinner I ate the last of the _____ meat, so tomorrow I must go out with the _____ and try to _____ something. I need more _____ for my lights, and also some _____ to make a new coat – this one is full of _____. But I am well and _____ – this island is my _____ now.

2 **Imagine that you have to spend a year alone on an island like Robinson Crusoe's. Explain why these things will, or will not, be useful on the island.**

Example: Matches will be useful for lighting fires.

a knife	chickens	a sword	salt	pen and paper
a tent	a bottle	a gun	money	matches

3 Here is a new illustration for the story. Find the best place in the story to put the picture, and answer these questions.

The picture goes on page _____.

1 What is Robinson Crusoe doing?
2 Why has Man Friday put his head on the ground?
3 Why doesn't Man Friday speak to Crusoe?

Now write a caption for the illustration.

Caption: _____

4 Put these words into four groups, under these headings.

| ANIMALS | PEOPLE | TRANSPORT | FOOD |

boat, bread, canoe, captain, corn, eggs, fruit, goat,
leopard, meat, pirate, prisoner, sailor, ship, slave, turtle

Now find these sixteen words in the word search below, and draw a line through them. The words go from left to right, and from top to bottom.

L	I	C	P	I	R	A	T	E	A
E	N	S	R	E	G	E	B	G	M
O	S	H	I	P	O	Y	R	G	S
P	F	C	S	L	A	V	E	S	A
A	R	B	O	A	T	O	A	U	I
R	U	N	N	T	R	Y	D	C	L
D	I	L	E	O	O	M	K	O	O
O	T	U	R	T	L	E	V	R	R
E	R	C	A	P	T	A	I	N	T
C	A	N	O	E	H	T	E	R	E

Now write down all the letters that don't have a line through them. Begin with the first line and go across each line to the end. You will have twenty-nine letters, which will make eight words, in two sentences.

1 Who said these two sentences?
2 Who was he talking to?
3 Where were they?

5 Here are Robinson Crusoe and the captain talking about the mutineers. Put their conversation in the right order, and write in the speakers' names. Crusoe speaks first (3).

1 _____ 'Leave them here. My island can be their prison.'

2 _____ 'That's true, you have. But how will they live?'

3 _____ 'What will you do with the mutineers, captain?'

4 _____ 'They won't escape easily, captain. Remember – I've been here for twenty-seven years.'

5 _____ 'I know that. But it's hard to kill so many men.'

6 _____ 'They can have my three houses, my cornfields, my goats, and all my tools. Their life will be easy.'

7 _____ 'I agree with you, my friend. But what can I do?'

8 _____ 'But they'll escape from it and go free!'

9 _____ 'Yes, it will. Ah, you're a kind man, Mr Crusoe.'

10 _____ 'I'll have to shoot them, Mr Crusoe. All mutineers must die, you know.'

6 There is a famous question about this story. Why was there only *one* footprint on the sand? Here are three possible answers. Which one do you like best, and why?

1 The man came to the shore in a boat, got out, put one foot on the sand, then got back into his boat again.

2 The man had only one leg.

3 There *were* other footprints on the sand, but the sea washed them away before Robinson Crusoe got there.

ABOUT THE AUTHOR

Daniel Defoe was born in London in 1660, the son of a butcher called James Foe (Daniel later changed his name to Defoe, because it was a more fashionable name). He went to a church school, and then went into business, buying and selling different things, and travelling all over Europe. He fought against one king (James II), and later joined the army of another king (William III). He went to prison twice because he wrote clever booklets against the church and the government. He travelled a lot, worked as a spy, started his own newspaper, and has more than 500 pieces of writing to his name – more than any other writer in the English language. It was a very full, busy, and exciting life. He died in 1731, in Ropemaker's Alley, London.

When he was nearly sixty years old, he began to write novels. These include *Captain Singleton*, *Moll Flanders*, and *Roxana*, but he is remembered best today for *Robinson Crusoe*. This was his first novel, written in 1719, and it was an immediate success. Defoe used the true story of a sailor called Alexander Selkirk, who was left by pirates on Juan Fernandez, a small island in the Pacific Ocean. He lived there alone for four years, and was rescued by a ship in 1709.

Many people call *Robinson Crusoe* the first English novel. It appears in many different languages, films are made of it, and the story of Crusoe on his island is still enjoyed today by both children and adults all over the world.

OXFORD BOOKWORMS LIBRARY

Classics • Crime & Mystery • Factfiles • Fantasy & Horror
Human Interest • Playscripts • Thriller & Adventure
True Stories • World Stories

The OXFORD BOOKWORMS LIBRARY provides enjoyable reading in English, with a wide range of classic and modern fiction, non-fiction, and plays. It includes original and adapted texts in seven carefully graded language stages, which take learners from beginner to advanced level. An overview is given on the next pages.

All Stage 1 titles are available as audio recordings, as well as over eighty other titles from Starter to Stage 6. All Starters and many titles at Stages 1 to 4 are specially recommended for younger learners. Every Bookworm is illustrated, and Starters and Factfiles have full-colour illustrations.

The OXFORD BOOKWORMS LIBRARY also offers extensive support. Each book contains an introduction to the story, notes about the author, a glossary, and activities. Additional resources include tests and worksheets, and answers for these and for the activities in the books. There is advice on running a class library, using audio recordings, and the many ways of using Oxford Bookworms in reading programmes. Resource materials are available on the website <www.oup.com/elt/gradedreaders>.

The *Oxford Bookworms Collection* is a series for advanced learners. It consists of volumes of short stories by well-known authors, both classic and modern. Texts are not abridged or adapted in any way, but carefully selected to be accessible to the advanced student.

You can find details and a full list of titles in the *Oxford Bookworms Library Catalogue* and *Oxford English Language Teaching Catalogues*, and on the website <www.oup.com/elt/gradedreaders>.

THE OXFORD BOOKWORMS LIBRARY
GRADING AND SAMPLE EXTRACTS

STARTER • 250 HEADWORDS
present simple – present continuous – imperative –
can/cannot, must – *going to* (future) – simple gerunds …

Her phone is ringing – but where is it?

Sally gets out of bed and looks in her bag. No phone. She looks under the bed. No phone. Then she looks behind the door. There is her phone. Sally picks up her phone and answers it. *Sally's Phone*

STAGE I • 400 HEADWORDS
… past simple – coordination with *and, but, or* –
subordination with *before, after, when, because, so* …

I knew him in Persia. He was a famous builder and I worked with him there. For a time I was his friend, but not for long. When he came to Paris, I came after him – I wanted to watch him. He was a very clever, very dangerous man. *The Phantom of the Opera*

STAGE 2 • 700 HEADWORDS
… present perfect – *will* (future) – *(don't) have to, must not, could* –
comparison of adjectives – simple *if* clauses – past continuous –
tag questions – *ask/tell* + infinitive …

While I was writing these words in my diary, I decided what to do. I must try to escape. I shall try to get down the wall outside. The window is high above the ground, but I have to try. I shall take some of the gold with me – if I escape, perhaps it will be helpful later. *Dracula*

STAGE 3 • 1000 HEADWORDS

... should, may – present perfect continuous – *used to* – past perfect –
causative – relative clauses – indirect statements ...

Of course, it was most important that no one should see
Colin, Mary, or Dickon entering the secret garden. So Colin
gave orders to the gardeners that they must all keep away
from that part of the garden in future. *The Secret Garden*

STAGE 4 • 1400 HEADWORDS

... past perfect continuous – passive (simple forms) –
would conditional clauses – indirect questions –
relatives with *where/when* – gerunds after prepositions/phrases ...

I was glad. Now Hyde could not show his face to the world
again. If he did, every honest man in London would be
proud to report him to the police. *Dr Jekyll and Mr Hyde*

STAGE 5 • 1800 HEADWORDS

... future continuous – future perfect –
passive (modals, continuous forms) –
would have conditional clauses – modals + perfect infinitive ...

If he had spoken Estella's name, I would have hit him. I was
so angry with him, and so depressed about my future, that I
could not eat the breakfast. Instead I went straight to the old
house. *Great Expectations*

STAGE 6 • 2500 HEADWORDS

... passive (infinitives, gerunds) – advanced modal meanings –
clauses of concession, condition

When I stepped up to the piano, I was confident. It was as if I
knew that the prodigy side of me really did exist. And when
I started to play, I was so caught up in how lovely I looked
that I didn't worry how I would sound. *The Joy Luck Club*

Huckleberry Finn

MARK TWAIN

Retold by Diane Mowat

Who wants to live in a house, wear clean clothes, be good, and go to school every day? Not young Huckleberry Finn, that's for sure.

So Huck runs away, and is soon floating down the great Mississippi River on a raft. With him is Jim, a black slave who is also running away. But life is not always easy for the two friends.

And there's 300 dollars waiting for anyone who catches poor Jim . . .

The Year of Sharing

HARRY GILBERT

Richard is bored with the quiet life of his village. He would like to have a motor-car and drive it . . . very fast. But Richard lives in a future world where there are no cars, only bicycles and small villages and green forests.

And now he is twelve years old, and like the other children, he must do his Year of Sharing. He must live alone in the forest with the wild animals. He must learn to share his world; he must learn how animals live and eat and fight . . . and die.